MENTORING MOMENTS WITH MYSELF

LETTERS TO MY YOUNGER SELF ABOUT LIFE, FAITH, LOVE AND LEADERSHIP

MICHELLE HOVERSON

Publishing services provided by  **Archangel Ink**

ISBN: 978-1-950043-07-1

Your Free Resource

Before you dive too far into this book, I have three exciting free bonuses to offer you:

1. The letter to self "Let Go" in a shareable pdf.

2. A going deeper piece on "Moving Beyond Unforgiveness."

3. Access to Mentoring Moments audio interviews as they are available.

To receive your free bonus content, sign up for the mailing list by visiting:

http://www.michellehoverson.com/book-bonus

Signing up will also notify you of any pending book releases or updated content. By subscribing you will be first in line for exclusive deals and future book giveaways.

Immediately after signing up you'll be sent an email with access to the bonus.

—Michelle

Endorsements

Reading *Mentoring Moments with Myself* is like spending time with a refreshingly honest, vulnerable, and seasoned life coach. Michelle shares wise words, offers space to breathe in their meaning, and creates room for reflection. In the midst of a complex world, this book is an invitation to sit back and savor simply stated principles and great advice.

> — Debbie O'Handley, executive director of Hope House

In *Mentoring Moments with Myself*, Michelle Hoverson offers a treasure trove of spiritual wisdom and insight that is personally reflective yet powerfully relevant to us all. The vulnerability she exhibits and the truths she expresses through challenging adult experiences compel us to examine our own shortcomings. I particularly like the Scripture references, meditative prompts, and journaling invitations to write mentoring messages to our younger selves and others.

> — Darryl L. Bego, Youth Development Initiatives

This book will take you on a journey, a roller-coaster ride of life, love, loss, and lessons. Michelle's letters will bring tears to your eyes, chuckles to your belly, and a clinching to your heart. Readers will encounter an opportunity to reset their course and an invitation to make God, Jesus, and the Holy Spirit the captain of their ship. Michelle's letters are chock-full of spiritual truths, aha moments, and gentle nudges to mentor you back into the arms of Jesus (where you, I, we belong). This is an essential mentoring book for cultivating Godly life skills. Grab your cup of coffee and settle in.

— Christi Ratcliff, success coach and speaker

As Christians, we are called to study the Word, to pray, and to seek out Godly counsel. *Mentoring Moments with Myself* embodies the latter of these commands. It offers retrospective wisdom to a younger self through faith-based principles derived from experience. Michelle Hoverson provides young Christian girls with a "back to the future" gift as she reflects upon her own faith-based journey. In today's fast-paced world, this book is a glimpse into what it takes to be a humble believer. It will surely draw you in, challenge you, and convict you to press forward. As a father of two daughters who were brought up in the church yet struggle with the realities of a postmodern world, I would strongly recommend that this book be offered as a gift to all young Christian women.

— Michael Arena, senior business executive and author of *Adaptive Space: How GM and Other Companies are Positively Disrupting Themselves and Transforming into Agile Organizations*

Do you ever think, *If only I knew then what I know now?* Join Michelle as she pours wisdom into her younger self and, by proxy, into her readers. Never again plead for a "do-over." You'll realize that we don't actually *have* to learn by doing but can benefit from the lessons of those who have gone before us. This little book can be read in one sitting, but I believe you'll find yourself coming back again and again to benefit from the life lessons Michelle candidly shares with her readers.

— Evan Stratton, founder of Strattegize

Contents

Acknowledgments

My heartfelt thank-you to...

My faithful number one fan, my husband, Walt, who never complained when I left him alone "to go upstairs and work on a letter." Walt, you are my sunshine.

John Edwards, who enthusiastically volunteered to do initial editing, knowing he would have to squeeze out the time to help me. John, you made me better.

My sister, Carol Cofer, who made the phone call after her morning time with the Lord and boldly encouraged me to step out and compile a book of letters.

John and Nita Youngblood, whose lifestyle of generosity and encouragement humbles me.

My forever sisters, Joy, Cory, Sandra, Rhonda, and Ingrid, who tenaciously asked me, "How's the book coming?" After your loving prodding, you always let me know you were praying.

Pastor Farrell Lemings, who invited me to speak at Grace Covenant on July 9, 2017, during the series on "Unsung Heroes." The message launched this book, which is just one of many God-sized doors I've walked through under his leadership.

The Above & Beyond board of directors, who blessed me

with their wholehearted support to pursue a dream. They are a gift from God.

All the people who have endured the results of my mistakes, wrong perspectives, and poor choices. You are part of these letters because you served as the threads in the tapestry of my life.

The Holy Spirit, the One who has faithfully inspired and instructed me since the day I invited Him to influence me in every aspect of life. He is my teacher, counselor, source of wisdom, and the One who drew me to give my life to Jesus. As you read these letters, if anything touches you, thank the Holy Spirit, for He whispered the words into my mind. I wouldn't want to live life without Him.

Introduction

Who do you most identify with in the Bible? I most identify with Peter, a disciple of Jesus. Many times, Peter acts first and processes later. I do that. Peter loves Jesus, but he doesn't always walk in a way that honors Him. Me too. Peter makes a couple of mistakes that are real doozies. Been there and have the T-shirt. Peter is always growing stronger in his faith and learning what's most important in life. I hope one day that will be said of me.

Personally, I think Peter gets a bad rap for losing faith and sinking in the water. What I most admire about the story of Peter walking toward Jesus on the water (Matthew 14:28–33) is that he tries to do something beyond his natural ability. He gets out of the boat when Jesus extends an invitation to come to Him. Does Peter fail? Yes, he does. But I admire Peter's courage to accept the unusual invitation.

In July 2017, I was invited to be a guest speaker at my home church, Grace Covenant. The church was in a series titled "Unsung Heroes," and I was assigned to speak on Jonathan and his faith risk recorded in 1 Samuel 14. I concluded the message by saying, "In the end, people most often regret the chances they failed to take—not the chances they took and failed." Then I shared a letter I had written to my younger self about risk. It's the first letter in the collection, titled "Go for It."

A friend posted a video of me reading the letter to the congregation on Facebook. I was shocked at how many people were sharing it with their friends and especially their daughters. I don't know the number that determines a video has gone viral, but I was astonished to see the video had been viewed by over 17,500 people. Friends, family, and acquaintances encouraged me to write more letters to my younger self on other topics. So I asked the Lord if by His Spirit He was inviting me to do something I had NEVER expected to do.

Peter wasn't a water-walker, and I am not a writer. You are holding in your hand a book written by a reluctant, slow, and insecure writer. By mid-2018, I realized I had received a divine invitation to step out of my comfort zone, trust God, and put pen to paper. I surrendered to the truth that His invitation wasn't based on how I see myself but on His greater perspective of who I can become. I've learned that when I accept the Lord's invitation to partner in something, He will add His super to my natural. Compiling these letters was definitely a project fueled by supernatural inspiration.

We live life forward, but we understand it looking backward. There are several ways we can gain perspective about life: We can read a good book, listen to a podcast, or attend a class addressing a life experience. Or we can learn from older relatives or mentors. Now that I am in my sixth decade, I've gained many perspectives about life. I'm hopeful that I can serve as that older mentor to you as I speak to my younger self.

Perhaps only one letter will speak to you now while another will come alive for you in a different season. One letter may help you avoid a misstep while another may encourage you that you are on the right track. Perhaps another letter will help a friend or family member as they consider a decision. Maybe, just maybe, there will be a letter that helps you take the chance and accept a divine invitation that has been extended to you.

I've read many books over the years and, other than my Bible, I don't return to many. But there are a few I revisit when I need counsel, inspiration, or encouragement. My prayer is that *Mentoring Moments with Myself* will become one of those books you revisit.

LETTERS

GO FOR IT

Dear One,

Your nature will be to seek comfort and safety. Yet you will be presented with some amazing uncharted opportunities.

Stepping into them will require a faith risk.

In an effort to avoid mistakes, you will want to retreat from making daring and bold moves. When you find yourself deliberating too long or waiting for one more sign from God, you will risk missing the miraculous if you choose safety and don't go up the mountain.

Don't wait for everything to be perfectly aligned to follow what God plants in your heart.

Make it your life's mission to know God. To step out in faith, you'll need to KNOW as much about Him as possible, and you'll need to know who you are *to* HIM. You will realize that your spiritual journey is more important than your earthly experiences.

Incoming messages will groom you to avoid failure. Yet, after rounding the last third of your life, you will realize that if you have attempted to trust God—even if you fail in the eyes of people—you will succeed in the eyes of the Lord.

Daring dependence on the Lord will be your highest accomplishment.

Go for it. Don't settle for less than a divine adventure.

Love,

Your Seasoned Self

Read and Reflect

Read the story of Jonathan in 1 Samuel 14:4–15.

The geographic descriptions given in 1 Samuel 14:4–5 refer to two steep crags on either side of a great ravine separating Geba on the south from Michmash on the north. Here Jonathan and his armor-bearer scaled the crags for a surprise attack on the Philistine garrison at Michmash. What gave Jonathan the confidence to "go for it" and take a risk facing overwhelming odds?

_____

_____

_____

_____

Have you ever declined a divine invitation to take a risk? Why do you think you were hesitant to "go for it"?

_____

_____

_____

_____

What do you want to tell your younger self about stepping out in faith to take a risk?

Dear Younger Me,

_____

_____

_____

_____

_____

_____

_____

_____

_____

_____

_____

_____

_____

_____

_____

CHAPTER 2 OR CHAPTER 22?

Dear One,

Comparison will be an ever-present trap.

After twenty-three years in full-time ministry through the church, you will set out to oversee the mission-oriented foundation Above & Beyond. You gave time to building the foundation while serving as Compassion Pastor in a large local church before the time came to jump in with both feet.

In the past, you inspired people to serve through programs. You cast vision and rallied others to causes. You served on leadership teams and established strategies. You wrote manuals, taught classes, designed brochures, and promoted ideas.

However, you have never raised money. This will take you swimming in the deep end of the pool.

Donor cultivation will be foreign territory. In fact, you've never led an organization without staff support and a senior leader providing guidance.

Faced with these realities, you will meet with people who have run nonprofits successfully, gleaning all kinds of ideas.

Then a pothole will flatten one of your tires.

Meeting with a friend who has led a massive international ministry, touching thousands of lives every year, you will ask, "How would you scale Above & Beyond if you were in my position?" Within the response you hear about millions of dollars raised, a prestigious board of directors that includes former NBA stars and media celebrities, a social media staff that is hitting the ball out of the park, hundreds of volunteers serving regularly, and annual planning retreats that produce volumes of creative ideas.

It's such a simple question, one you expect to produce a practical answer. Instead, the response will unleash a downward spiral of self-doubt. You will walk into his office with a bounce in your step but walk out wondering, *Why am I even trying this? I'm going to disappoint so many people. I don't know celebrities. I don't have any idea how to research a grant. I'm doing well to come up with three interesting Facebook posts a week.*

For about twenty-four hours, the conversation with your friend will haunt you.

Then, while pouring out your heart to the Lord, a thought will bubble up: *at one point, he was in your exact position…just starting.*

You will realize that your friend's nonprofit is experiencing chapter 22 in its development. You, however, are just writing your chapter 2.

Nothing will steal the hope and joy from your heart more quickly than comparison. Inferiority, inadequacy, insufficiency, and incompetence are just a few words to describe the feelings that arise when you compare yourself to someone's more advanced chapter. Envy and pride swell when you compare yourself to someone's lesser chapter.

When you engage in comparison, you miss celebrating what you have accomplished, and you rob others of valuable experiences you have to share. Both become rejected gifts.

Colossians 3:23–24 says, "Whatever you do, work at it with all your heart, as working for the Lord, not for human masters, since you know that you will receive an inheritance from the Lord as a reward. It is the Lord Christ you are serving." That's why a simple prayer like, "Lord, help me to be faithful where I am," will detach you from the web of comparison and free you to a renewed sense of purpose and contentment.

Later in the journey, and armed with a healthier perspective, you'll reflect upon a meeting with a lovely young lady who was writing chapter 1 of her ministry to orphans in Ethiopia. Since you will have moved into writing Above & Beyond's chapter 3 by then, it will be a greatly encouraging conversation for both of you.

Live free from the trap of comparison. Instead, allow others' successes to inspire you.

Celebrate the stories of others.

Celebrate yours too because you'll be writing your own chapter 22 one day.

Love,

Your Seasoned Self

Read and Reflect

Read Galatians 6:3-5 and Romans 12:3-8.

In what areas of life are you most tempted to fall into the comparison trap? How does comparison rob you?

_____

_____

_____

_____

_____

What unique gifts and abilities do you have that you are grateful for?

_____

_____

_____

_____

_____

What do you want to tell your younger self about avoiding the pitfalls of comparison and enjoying the current chapter?

Dear Younger Me,

_____

_____

_____

_____

_____

_____

_____

_____

_____

_____

_____

_____

_____

_____

_____

Note to Self

Achievements

As you are achieving goals and realizing successes, celebrate them, but remember: God cares more about the condition of your heart than the work of your hands. He desires that you become someone more than He wants you to do something. He longs for you to be filled with His Spirit so you will be a reflection of...

His grace.

His mercy.

His goodness.

His hope.

His compassion.

His love.

WHAT YOUR OBITUARY
SHOULD INCLUDE

Dear One,

On a summer day, you will find yourself sending this text to your husband:

> *I just want to thank you for always being faithful to me. I know of so many women right now who are struggling with the pain of unfaithfulness and I'm so grateful that in the last 29 years, I have not had one ounce of that discomfort.*

Faithfulness is fidelity, constancy, dependability, reliability, and loyalty. Its opponents are disloyalty, inconsistency, dishonesty, unreliability, and untrustworthiness.

Like being caught in the gale force winds of a hurricane, you will be dismantled emotionally when you experience the heartbreaking realities of unfaithfulness in your first marriage. The pain will feel unbearable.

Yet you will survive it. Although healing will come over time, there will be scar tissue.

Many see faithfulness as just a characteristic of a valued relationship, especially marriage. However, it's more than that. Faithfulness is a character attribute that impacts all aspects of life, family, work, and communion with God.

Because you have drunk from the bitter waters of past unfaithfulness, you will come to treasure the significance of faithfulness.

As you age, you will see culture slowly releasing its grip on the importance of faithfulness. We have become more and more comfortable making excuses for people who abandon ship when they think the grass is greener on the other side, the work environment is too demanding, or the wait for what they desire is too long.

Being faithful is doing the right thing consistently, day in and day out. That's not a sizzling description of a person, but it's an essential quality if you want to be respected and trusted.

This may seem like an odd story to share, but it's what comes to mind at the moment. A couple of years after college, in the late seventies, you'll find yourself driving a little sunshine-yellow Volkswagen Bug. It's what you can afford—simple, with absolutely no extras and an AM radio that only works sometimes. Forty years later, you'd love to own it again. At the time, though, you are a little embarrassed by its puttering and inconsistent heater. Because you don't really value that Bug, you aren't faithfully taking care of its basic service needs.

One Sunday, you hear a sermon focused on Luke 16:10 ("...whoever can be trusted with very little can also be trusted with much..."), and you have an aha moment. That yellow "jelly bean on wheels" will become an instrument in a life lesson. You will realize that if you faithfully take care of that small, insignificant car, you will demonstrate that you can be trusted with something better. After consistently keeping that car in pristine shape inside and out, you will secure a job that comes with a company car you could never afford on your own.

Faithfulness is rewarded.

Faithfulness is admired.

Faithfulness reaps the blessings of inner peace.

My seasoned counsel to you is to be:

...faithful to God.

...faithful in marriage.

...faithful to your core values.

...faithful in your assignments.

...faithful to your family and friends.

...faithful in your commitments.

...faithful to your lenders.

…faithful in prayer.

…faithful to your calling.

…faithful in the little things and when no one is looking.

Of all the words that could be written in your obituary, make sure you live in such a way that "she was faithful" is right up front.

Love,

Your Seasoned Self

Read and Reflect

Read Psalm 31:23, Proverbs 3:3-4, and Luke 16:10-12.

Why does God place a high value on faithfulness?

_____

_____

_____

_____

_____

_____

Why does unfaithfulness hurt so deeply?

_____

_____

_____

_____

_____

_____

What do you want to tell your younger self about the importance of faithfulness and what it means to be a faithful person?

Dear Younger Me,

_____

_____

_____

_____

_____

_____

_____

_____

_____

_____

_____

_____

_____

_____

_____

_____

_____

FRUITFULNESS OVER GREATNESS

Dear One,

A common message will be communicated to you from multiple directions and in various ways:

- Become great!
- Be the best!
- Don't settle for second best!
- Strive for the top!
- Be all you can be!

Maybe that's why your pride will swell when you are handed your White House pass. You'll think, *Now I am somebody.*

When you're invited to work on the largest account at the advertising agency, you will think, *I'm on my way to being the best.*

When the law firm asks you to become one of the first communications directors in the South, you'll think, *Finally, a position of importance.*

One would think you wouldn't carry the secret desire for greatness into ministry, but you will. Your need to have influence will be fed by more and more people filling the seats to hear what you share.

Greatness, achievement, accomplishment, importance, the need to be esteemed…all of these voices from your natural self will want to motivate you and influence your decisions.

The applause of man can become intoxicating, but don't drink the Kool-Aid. On the other side of the achievement addiction, you will find that striving for greatness isn't a worthy motivation. It brings no honor to God, is void of His blessing, and is toxic to your soul.

God gets your attention through Sister Gina. Ministering to people living in a garbage dump in Johannesburg, South Africa, she'll never know the critical role that she played in teaching you to set aside greatness.

While leading a mission team there, you will be invited to help her. Hundreds of people gather for a bowl of soup scooped from the big pots on the back of Sister Gina's pickup truck. Despite a lack of formal education, she obviously loves people and knows how to cook.

The Scriptures are her second language. She exhorts circles of people in an open-field church to worship. The power flows from her like water gushing from a fire hose.

To your amazement, hundreds of people who carved out shelter in the mounds of trash sing and praise God in what you can only describe as a taste of heaven. Something in you begins to break. As you yield to it, revelation comes. You realize that Sister Gina may not be great in the eyes of the world, but she is fruitful in the eyes of God.

Greatness is man's desire. Fruitfulness is God's desire for man.

To be fruitful means that you are reproducing the good fruit Christ has produced in you. The more you allow the Holy Spirit to operate in your life, the more fruitful you will be. Sister Gina produced abundant fruit because she abided in the Vine. The time she spent with God guaranteed that she was "fruit oriented," not "greatness oriented."

The neat thing about living to be fruitful is that you will eventually accomplish some amazing things. I'll let you in on a little secret about your life: the projects, the ministries, the conversations that will bring you the most joy are those that continue to produce fruit after you are gone.

Love,

Your Seasoned Self

Read and Reflect

Read John 15:1–11 and Galatians 5:22.

What is the key to being a fruitful person, according to these Scriptures?

_____

_____

_____

_____

_____

_____

What characteristics identify a fruitful life?

_____

_____

_____

_____

_____

_____

What do you want to tell your younger self about pursuing fruitfulness?

Dear Younger Me,

_____

_____

_____

_____

_____

_____

_____

_____

_____

_____

_____

_____

_____

_____

_____

_____

_____

Note to Self

Family Dysfunctions

Dysfunctional thinking and pain-producing behaviors will travel through a family until someone is brave enough to own them and deal with them. Instead of complaining, be the one with the courage to say, "I'll let the Lord sand me, shape me, and heal me so I'm the one to stop this muddy water flowing downhill to others."

GRATITUDE IS A GAME-CHANGER

Dear One,

Okay, I'm keeping it real. There is going to be a lot in life to complain about.

Your employers will annoy you, your spouse will disappoint you, kids will frustrate you, family will be family, taxes will infuriate you, aging will drive you to drink, and bank balances will perplex you.

You will have dozens of reasons daily—some good, some logical, and some socially acceptable—to grumble and complain.

Don't do it. Ungratefulness is socially unbecoming and spiritually limiting. No one is inspired by a grouch. You will do well to remember that the Israelites' eleven-day journey through the wilderness took forty years because of their ungratefulness.

We're told seventy-three times in the Bible to "give thanks." The older you has discovered why: gratitude changes our mental, emotional, and spiritual perspectives.

You will find yourself in many challenging situations, but a particularly difficult one is discovering that your son is dyslexic. The homework sessions will be tough for both of you. You'll spend a lot of money on specialists and private schools because you love him and want what's best for him. However, losing your savings will be disappointing, and watching him struggle will be disheartening.

When resentment, disappointment, and pity invite you to come out and play, don't go. Instead, give thanks and be grateful. You'll have a boatload of reasons to be grateful.

Be grateful that, because of the dyslexia, your son has developed a keen sense of justice and a heart of kindness. His creativity helps him to see the world in a way that's different from most, and you'll wish that his memory wasn't so well developed at times!

Be grateful for a husband who is partnering with you every step of the way.

Be grateful that, when you are afraid about your son's ability to learn and graduate, God will provide amazing tutors who enjoy seeing him succeed as much as you do.

Be grateful for the divine appointments when you "just happen to meet someone" that is an advocate for students with disabilities. Be grateful for the Scriptures that bring you hope, the people who pray for you and him, and the resources to provide for his needed extras. Be grateful that God saw abilities in you, entrusting your son into your care.

Not every day will be a good one, yet there will be goodness all around you every day. You might have to look for it. There will always be something to be grateful for. Every day you can choose to count your losses or count your blessings. Keep a gratitude journal and write down three things you are grateful for every day. As you focus on gratitude and thankfulness, joy will break loose from the ground of discouragement and discontentment.

Choose to live with gratitude. It's a game-changer.

Love,

Your Seasoned Self

Read and Reflect

Read Exodus 14, 1 Thessalonians 5:16–17, and Ephesians 5:20.

At times, we all find ourselves doing the same thing the Israelites did—complaining over inconveniences and discomforts. What are practical ways you can give thanks in the midst of unpleasant situations?

_____

_____

_____

_____

_____

_____

_____

_____

_____

What do you want to tell your younger self about gratitude and the dangers of ungratefulness?

Dear Younger Me,

_____

_____

_____

_____

_____

_____

_____

_____

_____

_____

_____

_____

_____

_____

_____

_____

_____

_____

Note to Self

Curb Your Stress

Stress is a fact of life, but you can curb its harmful effects. Keep your mind on what IS rather than being preoccupied with what MIGHT be. Delete the negatives: negative self-talk, negative people, negative news. Laugh—it's an instant vacation. Write a quick note of thanks. Pray for someone facing the same situation you are. Guard margin in your schedule; you are the only one who will. Schedule times to unplug and be still. You don't have to meditate to be still—walk in quiet or enjoy the first thirty minutes of the morning in silence. Live below your means. Stop talking about how stressed you are. When you feel overwhelmed, get out and get moving. Remind yourself that what you are so stressed about probably won't matter in a few weeks. It's amazing the things that just "work out," and if they don't, few people care. When all else fails, to keep stress in its proper place, just sing along to "Girls with Guitars" with Wynonna Judd!

IT WILL TAKE COURAGE

Dear One,

There will be times when you'll want to shrink back, wrap yourself up in a blanket, watch old movies, and eat chocolate. Yet you can't. You'll just have to muster courage and move forward.

In life, you will require courage to:

...be your authentic self.

...share your scars.

...age with grace and joy.

...walk by faith.

...consistently read the Scriptures.

...pray without ceasing.

...hold to biblical principles and not fade to gray.

...speak truth to those who have authority over you.

...call a thing a thing.

...accept God's grace and mercy.

...listen instead of lecture.

...stay faithful to your marriage vows.

…search for a solution instead of casting blame.

…deal with difficulties head-on and transparently.

…be okay with being respected rather than popular.

…build consensus instead of charging ahead.

…do the hard, yet right, thing when no one will ever congratulate you.

…let others take the credit, no more said.

…recognize that one day you will be part of the "older generation."

…let people express themselves and try to put your feet in their shoes.

…celebrate others' successes when you are discouraged.

…not have to win.

…let it go, and let them go.

…apologize and ask for forgiveness.

…say no and to say yes.

…let a failure influence you, not define you.

…accept that you can't always fix what you break.

…look for the lesson in a bad decision.

…stop trying to fit into places you've outgrown.

…stay in your own lane and not run the race someone else is winning.

…stop looking for satisfaction in the same place you lost it.

…take it one step at a time and not try to skip the steps.

…believe others' access to your heart is a privilege.

…embrace the tough experiences that have shaped you.

…disrobe from shame.

…live in the reality that you can't please everyone.

…admit that "good enough for now" is okay.

…empower others and give up control.

…be intentional.

…never give in to "Why bother anymore?"

…confront your insecurities and deal with them.

…laugh at yourself.

…accept a compliment, period.

…hold on to hope.

Being a courageous person isn't about running with the bulls or skydiving. Being courageous isn't about being a daredevil. It's about summoning the inner bravery to live the life you wake up to every day. Courage is a virtue, so be courageous.

Love,

Your Seasoned Self

Read and Reflect

Read Deuteronomy 31:6–8, Joshua 1:9–13, and Acts 3 and 4.

Why were Paul and John able to be courageous in the midst of great opposition?

_____

_____

_____

_____

_____

Where does courage come from?

_____

_____

_____

_____

_____

_____

What do you want to tell your younger self about the benefits and costs of exercising courage?

Dear Younger Me,

Note to Self

Words Matter

Taste your words before you spit them out. The Bible says that words carry the power to bring life or death, so pause before you speak. Once released, words can't be taken back. They are like seeds that drop into the heart of a person and produce either fragrant flowers and delicious fruit or weeds and briars. They create or destroy destinies. Before barking at someone, ask yourself "Would I want someone to speak to me in this way?" Speak wisely; don't toss words around carelessly. Be known as a person who speaks words that release nourishment, encouragement, hope, graciousness, and faith.

LOOSEN THE LASSO

Dear One,

Oh my gosh, you are going to make so many mistakes! Some will be minor, and others will be real doozies—Hall of Fame–level blunders.

There will be:

…the guy you date during your freshman year in college.

…the credit card debt in your thirties that you won't pay off until your forties.

…the commitment you make when your insides are screaming, *No, I don't want to do this!*

…the friend you trust who betrays your unzipped heart in ways you could never have anticipated.

…the job you don't take, and the one you take but shouldn't have.

The list could go on for pages and pages. The point of this letter isn't to criticize but to focus on what you will learn.

You will learn that you can't allow your mistakes, errors of judgment, and wrong choices to lasso you. Your past is your past, and you can't live by looking through the rearview mirror. We gain understanding by looking backward, but God made us to live in forward motion, to set our sights on the horizon before us and not the one behind.

The consequences of your past experiences will *affect* you, but they don't have to *infect* you with a failure identity. After your divorce, you will tell yourself (and others will suggest) that you're "damaged goods and a failure." It won't be true. Shame will always try to set up camp in your mind if you let it. Shame wants to dismantle your confidence by diverting your focus from who you are to how you failed.

Don't let your past *define you,* let it *refine you*. As you yield your mistake-riddled life to God, He will sand you, reshape you, heal you, and show Himself to you. When the messy season closes, you will overflow with a new level of grace and compassion for others who have "blown it."

Some mistakes and wrong decisions will be easier to let go of than others. Regardless, they are all in the past. If you allow yourself to be lassoed to the past, you will never be free to live fully in the present. That rope around your neck will pull you back at random moments and you will slip back into the corral of regrets. You will never move forward if you are circling in the corral filled with "What ifs" and "I shouldn't haves."

On the cross, Jesus paid for your poor choices and mistakes. Since He purchased your freedom from the weight of condemnation and shame, don't allow the Accuser of the Brethren to lasso you with past guilt.

Take the lasso off.

Run free.

Love,

Your Seasoned Self

Read and Reflect

Read Isaiah 43:18–19, John 18:13–27, and John 21:15–18.

How could Peter's life have been different if he'd lived in his past mistake?

_____

_____

_____

_____

_____

Why is it hard to let go of failures and not allow them to define us?

_____

_____

_____

_____

_____

_____

What do you want to tell your younger self about failure and living beyond your mistakes?

Dear Younger Me,

_____

_____

_____

_____

_____

_____

_____

_____

_____

_____

_____

_____

_____

_____

_____

_____

_____

_____

_____

Note to Self

Facing Trials

You will face serious trials: relationships fracture, natural disasters arrive unexpectedly, business plans go south, health is jeopardized. Regardless of the nature of the difficulty, remember this: trials test our trust. Are you going to put your trust in your ability to fix things, or are you going to place the situation in God's hands and trust Him to lead you through the valley...no matter how long it takes?

When you enter a trying season, encourage yourself to...

trust God to do the impossible.

trust God for a "suddenly."

trust God to make all things new.

trust God to guide you.

trust God to protect you.

trust God to see you through.

*trust God to cause opportunities
to arise out of adversity.*

trust God to turn misery into ministry.

trust God to do what you can't.

*Trust no matter what storm comes, no
matter when the storm strikes, and no
matter where you find yourself when the
storm hits. God is with you—Immanuel.*

MANNERS WILL MATTER

Dear One,

When you hear this voicemail message, you'll shake your head in fresh wonder:

> *I can't believe you wrote a thank-you note by hand. I haven't received one of these in years. Thank you for thanking me.*

Although it takes just a few minutes to write a simple thank-you note, it's rare to receive one.

In many ways, cordiality is disappearing under the tide of ever-growing social media posts and text messaging. Some may think that manners represent an outdated way of thinking and etiquette is a custom of the past or a tradition reserved for royalty.

It simply isn't true.

Manners are more than fussy rules enforced by fussy people. Manners are the oil that lubricates culture to reduce friction in relationships. Manners either attract or distance people.

Although the State Department's Social Secretary position will always be a dream job, you'll find that you don't need a platform to be considerate. Politeness will never be passé. Rudeness will always be rooted in selfishness.

More importantly, the disciplines of courtesy, sensitivity to others' feelings and culture, and respect for authority and diverse opinion should mark your life as a Christian.

You will never avoid manners malpractice perfectly, but you will learn some practical "manners that matter." Practice these as a way of life.

- Be kind. The world is harsh.

- Smile. It can make a big difference in someone's day.

- Never return a dish empty. Include something as simple as a piece of candy.

- Respond quickly to an invitation. There is nothing more frustrating for a host than not knowing how many guests to anticipate.

- Curb and clean up after your dog.

- Be the neighbor that you want for a neighbor.

- Before complaining about others, remember that *you* can be a real jerk too.

- Prevent children from referring to an adult by their first name. Adults are not their peers.

- Honor and show deference to senior adults. In many ways, they have paved the path for you. Remember: someday you will be in the senior class.

At a dinner table:

- Learn to use flatware properly. Navigating a table setting will give you confidence in a wide range of social situations.

- If you are seated at a table with eight guests or fewer, wait until everyone is served before lifting your fork. It's a sign of respect.

- While enjoying your meal, keep anything off the table that's not food related. Your phone is not a table guest.

- Read a good etiquette book to learn basic table manners.

While communicating with others:

- "Please," "Thank you," and "Excuse me," should be key phrases in your vocabulary.

- Say "yes" instead of "yeah."

- Express your appreciation for someone's generosity or kindness. Although sending a text is better than no communication, sincere appreciation is better expressed in a handwritten thank-you note. Relationships are worth the cost of a stamp and a piece of paper.

- Teach your children how to write thank-you notes early in their lives so it becomes a habit.

- In a public setting, use headphones when watching a video or listening to music.

- Reciprocate while replying to the common question, "How are you?" or "How is your family?"

- Learn good questions to ask people about themselves. If you do, you'll always be able to hold a conversation with someone you've never met.

- Introducing people to each other makes encounters less awkward.

- Always let the other person know if a telephone conversation is taking place on speakerphone.

- Honor people's family and/or personal time. Be mindful of what time it is when you are texting and calling.

- Listen.

- If someone has earned a PhD or medical license, refer to him/her as "Doctor." Such achievement deserves respect.

About money:

- If you borrow someone's vehicle, put gas in it.

- If you borrow money, pay it back before it's expected.

- When you are the guest in someone's home, go out of your way to minimize the host's cost.

- Practice reciprocity, charity, and generosity.

While traveling:

- If you're boarding an aircraft, don't wear strong cologne or creams.

- If you must get up during a flight, don't pull the back of the seat in front of you in the process.

- Go with the flow in hallways, sidewalks, and airport terminals. If you must send a text message or email while on a moving sidewalk in airport terminals, move to the side.

- When staying at the home of a friend or family member, be helpful and offer to take used linens to the laundry room. When it comes to sleepwear, choose modesty. Return items to their original location. Only show up with a child or pet if you've cleared it with your host in advance.

- Don't remove makeup on the host's light-colored towels. Carry wipes or ask for a paper towel.

- Always ask a host, "Where's a good place to change the baby?"

- Before traveling internationally, research cultural differences, especially in relation to etiquette. Never assume the way we do it in the U.S. is the "right way" in another country.

In the workplace:

- Don't microwave pungent foods.

- Arrive on time for appointments. Punctuality is an expression of respect for another person's time.

- Return phone calls and emails promptly. As needed, simply let the sender know that you won't have an answer for a while. Don't leave him/her in limbo by your silence.

- Avoid using ALL CAPS in an email unless you want the recipient to think you are screaming.

- Ask someone if he/she has time to speak to you. Don't assume it.

- Focus on being fully present during meetings. It is disrespectful to check your personal device or respond to emails during that time. Wouldn't you like to have another person's attention if you were speaking?

- If you are sick, stay home. Your colleagues will thank you.

- Silence your phone during meetings.

- If you can't write a good recommendation for a coworker, encourage the person to ask someone else.

- Ask what the appropriate attire is. Never assume that what you like to wear is what you should wear.

Since you won't live in isolation on another planet, remember that your actions, habits, communications, and behavior affect others. Manners matter.

Love,

Your Seasoned Self

Read and Reflect

Read Matthew 7:12, 1 Corinthians 13:5, Ephesians 4:29, Colossians 4:5, and 1 Peter 3:15.

Why should a follower of Christ exhibit good manners?

_____

_____

_____

_____

_____

Are there areas of manners malpractice you need to correct?

_____

_____

_____

_____

_____

What do you want to tell your younger self about the difference between a life sensitive to manners compared to one disregarding manners?

Dear Younger Me,

_____

_____

_____

_____

_____

_____

_____

_____

_____

_____

_____

_____

_____

_____

_____

_____

_____

_____

_____

THE AGING ADVANTAGE

Dear One,

Age is just a three-letter word. What matters is how you are aging. Life has no rewind button, so make your life count at every age.

The more you age, the more you realize:

...the importance of knowing when to remain silent.

...the responsibility of speaking the truth in love dipped in grace.

...the significance of recognizing situations that no longer require your time, energy, and focus.

...the value of the pause: when in doubt—pause; when making a big decision—pause; when angry—pause before responding; when tired—pause before reacting. And when you pause—pray.

...the cost of not walking away from toxic people.

... the importance of believing your current situation is not your final destination.

...the truth that you are not too old, it's not too late, and life is much shorter than you imagined.

...the reality that you can do nothing of lasting significance without being connected to the Father, Son, and Holy Spirit.

...the fact you can spend a lot less, own less, live with less, and be perfectly content.

...the inevitability of change and the importance of embracing it and navigating it in a healthy way.

...the fact that time does not heal all wounds, but the Holy Spirit does—if you engage the process.

...the importance of treating your family with care. When push comes to shove, you will want them near you.

...the understanding that pain produces purpose and even gives birth to passion.

...the acceptance that we must climb hills to develop endurance and visit the valley of tears to cultivate compassion.

...the fact that all those people you thought were thinking about you weren't.

...the need to, every now and then, just turn around, throw the match, and burn the bridge.

...the reality that we are never the sole author of our accomplishments. Honor and acknowledge those who have been part of your success.

...the need to beware of the drift. A little grazing here, a little distraction there, pressure at work, sick family members, and one day you'll realize you've wandered from the Lord and the people and principles that are most important to you.

...the blessing is sometimes not getting what you want and pray for.

...the importance of living generously and fighting against the sense of scarcity. Even when resources are tight, you can always be generous with your service, hospitality, and encouraging words. You will always have something you can give away.

...the liberty in not feeling like you have to explain why you are saying no.

...the reality that most of what you worried about never came to pass.

...the difference it would have made if you had prayed more and worried less.

...the understanding that God doesn't always deliver us the way we pray He will. Sometimes He removes us from a situation. Other times He strengthens and develops us in the midst of the situation. Other times He liberates us from this world and brings people to their eternal home.

Aging isn't something to resent. Aging is God's plan, so celebrate its finer points. The wrinkles may grow in number, and gravity may take its toll, but the wisdom and contentment that will come alongside them are gifts to be treasured.

Love,

Your Seasoned Self

Read and Reflect

·

Read Ruth 4:15, Psalm 92:12–15, Proverbs 16:31, Isaiah 46:4, and Job 12:12.

What promises does the Lord make to us as we age?

_____

_____

_____

_____

_____

What fears about aging do you need to give to the Lord?

_____

_____

_____

_____

_____

What do you want to tell your younger self about embracing aging and its advantages?

Dear Younger Me,

_____

_____

_____

_____

_____

_____

_____

_____

_____

_____

_____

_____

_____

_____

_____

_____

_____

_____

Note to Self

Parenting

Parenting is a privilege, and you are responsible to the Creator for how you shepherd the lambs He gives you. You are raising a child to become an emotionally healthy contributing adult who one day will find an emotionally healthy contributing adult to partner with in life. Give up trying to be a perfect parent. No one has achieved that distinction. Parenting is an imperfect pursuit. Guilt always creeps into parenting. Don't waste emotional energy on guilt. Do your best to show your child you love them and are for them. Get to know them. Value their uniqueness and don't try to box them into what you want them to become. Introduce your child to God, and when they drift, trust God's love for them to bring them close again. Keep a journal of all the funny things your child says. You think you won't forget, but you will. Maximize car time together; see what great conversations might come up. Make family dinners a priority. They keep everyone connected. Remember, with God's help, you can do this!

WHO TO MARRY

Dear One,

Deep in your heart, you will sense that the man waiting at the altar is not God's best for you. Minutes before you enter the church on your wedding day, your father will whisper, "You don't have to do this."

You'll have permission to make a U-turn.

Yet as your father squeezes your hand, awaiting a response, tumbling thoughts will expose deep insecurity and fear:

What will others say?

How do I return the gifts?

Is there any other man who would want to marry me?

Can I do this to him?

Unfortunately, you will reach this conclusion: *I need to do this. I mean…I love him and I want to do this.*

The experience of your first marriage will be like a summer tan—everything looks good on the front, but the backside needs a lot of work. Although you enjoy your husband's company, there will be flaws in the bedrock of his character.

You will think you can change him, but you can't. Although others will sense days of heartbreak approaching, you keep hoping that he will want to change and seek help because of how much he loves you. Oprah Winfrey describes how the late Maya Angelou counseled her, "When people show you who they are, believe them."[1] Oprah added, "Believe them the first time. Don't wait for the twenty-ninth time." How true.

At this life stage, you won't understand that transformation begins only when a person decides that he or she wants to change.

Denial will hold the upper hand in your life. Never wanting to be a member of the "Failed-Marriage Club," you will desperately want this man to love you (which really means "change for you").

You will learn many lessons in this ugly season of life. One is, a man can capture your eye while hiding things in his heart. Another is, despite what a man says to you, how he treats you is how he really feels about you.

It's important to celebrate that someone wonderful came from your error in judgment, since your first husband is the father of your son. The point of this

1 – Oprah's Life Class, "When People Show You Who They Are, Believe Them," OWN, Aired on 10/26/2011, video, 3:44, http://www.oprah.com/oprahs-lifeclass/when-people-show-you-who-they-are-believe-them-video.

letter is not to criticize but to share what you will learn regarding the man you should marry.

If you marry with the wrong motivation, count on a wrong outcome. Your first marriage will be a painful example. An enormous amount of self-doubt causes you to see his proposal as a validation of your worth. Only in hindsight do you see it's such a flawed reason to say yes.

Low self-perception and need for acceptance can never be resolved by someone else. But your divorce compels you to spend time on introspection, inner healing, and becoming a better you. During the process, a thought finally clicks: *healthy people attract healthy people*.

A smart girl emerges from that refining fire.

Your next marriage will be lovely, an adventure beyond your imagination and currently eclipsing three decades.

Through the wrong and right choices, you'll learn that it's critical to:

…marry God's man for you. Walking closely with the Lord is the foundation for identifying your life partner.

…marry the man who wants to grow in his relationship with the Lord.

…marry the man who adds value to your life. When you are together, it needs to be a great "us."

...marry the man who is genuinely interested about your day.

...marry the selfless man who serves others without being asked.

...marry the helpful man who supports you as you grow through what you go through.

...marry the listening man who just lets you talk.

...marry the cheerleading man who encourages you to be your best.

...marry the man who challenges you but never condemns you.

...marry the man who speaks respectfully about other women.

...marry the authentic man, the one you're safe to be yourself with, because he is willing to share his vulnerabilities with you.

...marry the confident man who isn't afraid to be himself and isn't competing with you.

...marry the man who attracts animals.

...marry the man who respects his mother but will not place her before you.

...marry the resolute man who will stand up for what he believes and will stand up for you.

...marry the man of integrity who does the right thing when no one sees it.

...marry the man who shares your core values and non-negotiable principles.

...marry the man willing to compromise—who likes to win but doesn't have to.

...marry the man with friends, especially friends that have journeyed with him awhile.

...marry the man who can laugh, especially at himself.

...marry the man who winks at you from across the room.

...marry the man who despises secrets.

...marry the man who will pray for you.

...marry the man who loves you but loves God more.

If every box is checked, it won't guarantee a conflict-free relationship or insulate you from stormy seasons. However, these characteristics describe the kind of man who will faithfully navigate the storms of life with you.

You will learn that the man you marry can be very different from you in personality, food preferences, interests, tastes in music and décor, etc. These differences will make life interesting and spark engaging conversations. In fact, these differences will hone your negotiation skills.

More important than heritage, wealth, social background, looks, popularity, and education will be a man's *character*. How he deals with everyday situations, as well as extraordinary pressures and temptations, will reveal the depth of his character. His perseverance and priorities will be revealed through his character. So don't rush to a conclusion about him. Give yourself time to see him in a variety of situations so you can observe his character.

When you're moving together toward the sunset of your lives, you won't relish what he bought or where you've been. What will mean the most to you, what you will want to share in his eulogy, is that he was a devoted follower of Christ, a loving father, a faithful partner, and your number one fan.

Marry that man.

Love,

Your Seasoned Self

Read and Reflect

Read Proverbs 13:1-6, 10-11, 15-18; and Matthew 7:24-27.

What are five critical qualities you look for in a mate? Do you possess these qualities?

_____

_____

_____

_____

_____

Why do people marry the person they should not?

_____

_____

_____

_____

_____

What do you want to tell your younger self about how to prepare to marry the right person and avoid marrying the wrong person?

Dear Younger Me,

THE CHOICE IS YOURS

Dear One,

As children and teenagers, we desire independence. Yet little do we know the incredible responsibility that comes with making our own choices.

Of course, we don't get to make choices about every aspect of our lives. For example:

- God chooses the time of our birth.
- Parents choose where we grow up and the family dynamics that shape us.
- Educational systems and teachers choose information designed to develop our minds.
- Coaches choose whether to place us on teams and how much we play.
- Employers choose whether to hire or fire.
- Governments choose laws to enact.
- Genetics chooses proclivity to conditions.
- God chooses an exit date.

Similarly, you won't have the opportunity to choose others' attitudes, whether someone accepts your apology, the health of those you love, your neighbors, the air conditioning unit's breakdown in the middle of summer, the person sitting next to you on a flight, your coworkers…and many more realities of life.

Although many choices will be beyond your control, life will offer an infinite number of possibilities. Some will be insignificant, such as choosing a certain day's lunch or the color to paint your bedroom. Others could lead to unerasable mistakes, such as choosing to have another glass of wine before driving or giving your heart to the wrong person. Sometimes choices aren't clearly best or worst. Sometimes you must choose between multiple good options, or you have to make a choice when none of the options are desirable. Regardless of the type of choice you're making, the direction of your life will reflect your choices.

Eighteen months into your first marriage separation, you will face a major choice in a moment's time that will affect a lot of people.

After your husband chooses to leave, you and your three-year-old son will move from Virginia to Atlanta for a time of recalibration. You will learn that your husband's choices have left you with a seemingly insurmountable mountain of debt. You'll make a beneficial choice to liquidate assets and move in with siblings.

After working hard and making great sacrifices for a year to pay off debt, the fateful time will come to meet with an accountant about taxes. When he shares the consequences of selling certain assets to pay debts, your reaction will make the phrase "shell-shocked" seem mild.

As you walk to your car like a wounded animal, the devil smells opportunity. He knows you're tapped out, barely keeping up with basic provisions. The battle for your mind begins as thoughts swarm:

You'll never pay this off.

The interest is going to mount and mount.

This is so unfair.

I've been trying to do the right thing. How could this happen to me?

What am I going to do? I'm out of options.

About halfway home, the mother of all thoughts attacks: *With my life insurance policy, I'm worth more dead than alive. Travis would be cared for well, and all these problems would come to an end.*

Losing hope can be deadly.

As these insidious thoughts try to take root, you will take your hands off the steering wheel and close your eyes.

When the car drifts from the right lane of the interstate toward the roadside banking, there will come another thought. This one isn't from your mind; it rises up from deep within you: *What about all the people you have told about Jesus? What are they going to think about your death? Faces and names appear before your eyes.*

In a split second, you will choose life.

Screaming "NO!" you will grab the wheel, steer back onto the road, and pull off at the next exit. In a parking lot, you will wage a spiritual battle in prayer. Like never before, you'll turn into a scriptural machine gun, firing relentlessly at the adversary of your soul and declaring the promises of God for your life.

It will prove to be a defining moment; you will have made a life-shaping choice.

Your life will be marked by thousands of day-to-day choices. Whether potentially life-altering or relatively insignificant, it's important to realize that:

…life will not be fair. Choose to count your blessings, not your losses.

…life will be short. Choose to burn the candles, use nice sheets, and buy fancy lingerie. Every day you awaken is a special day.

…aging will be unavoidable. Choose to embrace the process and even celebrate it.

…people will mistreat you, discount your opinion, and disrupt your life. Some will intend to hurt and others won't. Regardless of their motives, choose to forgive and don't let resentment take root in your heart.

…people will disagree with your perspective. Choose to listen to theirs. When appropriate, challenge without arguing.

…if you take risks, you will fail. Choose to see each failure as a stepping-stone to success. Choose to brand yourself as an overcomer, not label yourself as a failure.

…everyone has bad days. Choose to get up, dress up, and show up the next day and the next.

…you have weaknesses. Choose to develop your strengths.

…when monetary resources become challenging, choose to be generous.

…blessings will come. Choose to be grateful, giving without expecting.

…people will pressure you to conform. Choose to be a prototype, not a stereotype.

…shortcuts will seem very attractive. Choose to take the long road and do the right thing.

…complaining will be easy. Choose to seek solutions instead.

...there will be valleys. Choose to press on because it's in the valleys where lilies grow.

...BIG challenges will come. Choose to place your confidence in God and do not retreat in fear.

...decisions must be made. Choose to let God's Word guide you more than your feelings and desires.

...others will enjoy success and accomplishments you were hoping to achieve. Choose to celebrate with them and neutralize envy.

...the world can be harsh and cruel. Choose to be kind.

...you'll weather seasons where you feel you're continually on the losing side. Choose to awaken the warrior within and not wallow in self-pity.

...some issues will be complicated. Choose to be a critical, creative, and independent thinker.

...inborn talents and learned abilities are gifts. Choose to develop them but put your faith in God.

...no organizations—not even churches—are perfect. Choose to remain engaged, affecting change rather than walking away.

...family members are important. Choose to do what it takes to maintain relationships, since you will want them near "when push comes to shove."

…sometimes situations will look impossible. Choose to believe that miracles happen every day. Choose prayer over worry.

…expenses will come up unexpectedly. Choose to live below your means.

…the Holy Spirit is real and active. Choose to partner with Him.

…people will try to inject their drama into your life. Choose to decline these invitations.

…jobs will change. Choose to finish well.

…people will flow in and out of your life. Choose your close friends wisely.

…God will reveal His Word and His ways. Choose to obey and apply, not discount what He reveals.

…the Holy Spirit will be gracious to warn you. Choose to yield to that flashing yellow light within.

…everyone has past junk that influences their present. Choose not to be judgmental, taking time to hear a person's story.

…happiness will not be a permanent state. Choose wholeness and health.

…while earning a living will be a necessity, choose to view work as a privilege and a divine assignment.

...dreams will be deposited into the heart. Choose to pursue them. If you have to place them on a shelf labeled "someday," it doesn't mean they won't come to pass.

...the mind will be prone to forget. Choose to read this list often.

Above all, choose to live by Proverbs 3:5–6: "Trust in the Lord with all your heart and lean not on your own understanding; in all your ways submit to him and he will make your paths straight."

Love,

Your Seasoned Self

Read and Reflect

Read the Book of Proverbs.

Why do choices shape our destiny?

_____

_____

_____

_____

_____

What is the most life-defining choice you have made?
Would you make the same choice today? If not, why?

_____

_____

_____

_____

_____

What do you want to tell your younger self about how
good choices are made?

Dear Younger Me,

_____

_____

_____

_____

_____

_____

_____

_____

_____

_____

_____

_____

_____

_____

_____

_____

Note to Self

Surrender

The world will inspire you with all kinds of messages to elevate your confidence in yourself. "Believe it and you can be it." "You are the master of your ship." "You are the curator of your life." "If you can imagine it you can become it."

These quotes sound great. They stir the soul and are encouraging. However, they are misleading. You were created to trust in Someone much greater than yourself. You were created to trust God—with everything. The years chasing after self-significance are wasted days. You will never find fulfillment, contentment, or confidence until you surrender yourself to the One who created you. It's an amazing truth that you will only find yourself when you surrender yourself (Matthew 10:39 and 16:25).

YOUR BOAT IS TOO COMFORTABLE!

Dear One,

When Jesus encountered future disciples and said, "Follow me," imagine what they would have missed if one replied, "Thanks, but I'm comfortable catching fish. I think I'll just stay close to my boat."

Staying in place can rob you of a fulfilling life.

Do you remember when you tried to ride a bike for the first time? You were scared silly when the training wheels came off. Yet your newfound freedom to explore the neighborhood was worth it!

In the same way, you will be stuck in your comfort zone for most of your life unless you allow disruptions. As your comfort zone breeds complacency, that can lead to catastrophe. Think about marriages where two people grew apart because they became complacent.

Within established routines, you won't learn much. It will feel awkward to change things. However, when you step daringly into the unknown, the story of your life will become interesting. You might feel like an idiot for a few minutes, but you don't have to know everything in advance to experience something new.

For example, amazing things will happen when you disrupt your comfort zone and say yes to serving on a mission team. While taking the step to serve in an unknown culture, share a room with a stranger, and eat unfamiliar food, God will break into your life in a new way. You will be invigorated by different worship styles. You'll be inspired by fresh perspectives on the Scriptures. Gratitude and love will awaken as your heart becomes entwined with others in ways you could never have imagined. Serving will bring satisfaction. Your heart will be changed by a new way of seeing God at work. You will bloom.

The more you step beyond the routines, the less scary it becomes to disrupt your comfort zone.

As you journey through life, you will realize that not everyone sees the world like you and your inner circle. Although it may be comfortable to flock with those who share the same interests, spiritual beliefs, and political viewpoints, that will prevent you from growing. While it will be challenging to engage with someone extremely different from you, it will bring great rewards. Your critical thinking will become broader and sharper.

Although everyone is made in the image of God, our culture likes to polarize people into us versus them. You will sense a natural "tug" to view those with different cultural imprints and belief systems as too odd to relate to or, worse, enemies. However, if you will disrupt your comfort, you will discover that meeting new and different people adds zest and imagination to what could have been a dull, routine, and comfortable life.

So, bite the bullet. Rise up. Summon courage. Take a step of faith. Shake things up.

Rearrange the furniture. Try the new lipstick color. Tap your creative side. Sign up for the class. Go to lunch alone with a book. Drink coffee at a new place. Strike up a conversation with a total stranger. Attend a different church one Sunday. Listen to new music or read a book that you don't think you'll like. Be a tourist and explore an area of town on your own. Cook with a foreign spice. Order from a different section of the menu. Take an alternate route to work. Brush your teeth with the opposite hand. Do something that scares you.[2]

When you make decisions, don't think only in terms of what you like or dislike. There's a third option: TRY. Try something new every week.

Face your discomfort.

God's plan for you will always be bigger than your limited perspective. Endurance is not His sole plan for your life.

Because life, in all its fullness, is a wonderful gift from God, step out of the "comfortable" boat.

Love,

Your Seasoned Self

---

2 – For example, write a collection of letters to your younger self for others to read!

Read and Reflect

Read the Book of Ruth and Matthew 14:22–33.

What would Ruth and Peter have missed if they had stayed in the familiar and not stepped out of their comfort zone?

_____

_____

_____

_____

_____

In what area of life do you need to challenge yourself to leave your comfort zone?

_____

_____

_____

_____

_____

What do you want to tell your younger self about disrupting comfort zones?

Dear Younger Me,

_____

_____

_____

_____

_____

_____

_____

_____

_____

_____

_____

_____

_____

_____

_____

_____

LET GO

Dear One,

A vast number of books and articles have been written about forgiveness.

There's a good reason.

You will realize that extending forgiveness to others is one of the most difficult and important things you will ever do for yourself. The degree to which you are willing to release resentment, bitterness, and offense will affect the degree to which you experience inner contentment, peace, and joy. It's a critical decision!

When a human heart is robbed of blood flow, that person will eventually gasp for air. The same is true with a blockage in your spiritual/emotional heart. When unforgiveness is lodged in your heart, you can't function at full capacity. Unforgiveness blocks the flow of God's grace.

Where His grace is limited, life is limited...and God is all about life. Jesus talks about it in John 10:10, "The thief comes only to steal and kill and destroy; I have come that they may have life, and have it to the full."

Like a thief, unforgiveness will rob you of the fullness of life He came to make possible.

People will hurt you, betray you, deceive you, and reject you. Count on it. They will cut your heart, bruise your ego, and stomp upon your dreams. You'll be angry. You'll even feel a desire for revenge.

These are natural responses. In itself, anger isn't a sin. After all, Jesus got angry. Yet it's when this natural emotion ferments and turns to resentment or bitterness that a systemic virus contaminates you, your future, and those around you.

Forgiveness, letting go of your prideful sense of justice to set someone free from retribution, is the only remedy for this toxic infection. A forgiving person is never jailed by the pain of the other person's violation.

Forgiveness may not be deserved. That's not the point because forgiveness is about releasing mercy. As you let go of the offender, you will realize that the offending individual will no longer have the power to traumatize you over and over again. It's a clean break from whatever chains you to the past, freeing your journey into the future.

You can transfer the execution of justice to our Righteous God, knowing that you have been forgiven so much.

C.S. Lewis, the great Christian writer, penned it this way: "To be a Christian means to forgive the inexcusable because God has forgiven the inexcusable in you."[3] God paid the high price of His Son, Jesus, so that you could be forgiven of every past, present, or future transgression, even before you had a true relationship with your Creator. When your life was rooted in self-centered destruction, with no way out, God loved you *that* much. Knowing how much mercy has flowed to you, how can you withhold it from others?

To be a forgiving person you will need to believe:

...choosing to forgive is obedience to the Scriptures. Nurturing unforgiveness is disobedience.

...forgiveness is a lifestyle, not a one-time choice. Forgive endlessly.

...forgiveness is not condoning or making excuses for another person, eliminating consequences, or giving permission to cause additional harm or rewrite history.

...Christ-followers are called to be agents of reconciliation, making forgiveness a high calling.

...mercy and love are poured back into you when you pour them out. They're hallmarks of a forgiving person.

If you wait for your emotions to give you permission to forgive, you may wait a long time. After all, it's

---

3 – C. S. Lewis, *The Weight of Glory* (New York: Harper Collins, 2009).

counterintuitive. It is an absolute yet perplexing truth that you are liberated when you release another person from the sentence of his/her wrongdoing.

Your feelings will tell you that some hurts are too large, yet Jesus' command to forgive doesn't include a list of exceptions. Living as a forgiving person will be easier when you realize that Jesus forgave others for much more serious offenses than what you are wrestling with.

Here's some great news: When you choose to forgive, you won't have to do it in your own strength. The Holy Spirit is with you and will help you through the process.

It's easy to quickly forgive people who hurt you with a "paper cut" offense. A deeper work of forgiveness will be required for those who impale you at the core of your being. This kind of forgiveness happens over time, and that's okay. The Holy Spirit will guide you through each step and show you every detail that needs to be released. As you engage in the process, you will eventually realize that you are no longer in pain. The hurt will become part of your history and pain will release its power over you. A time will come when you will know that you have forgiven completely.

Sometimes, the hardest person to forgive will be yourself. Instead of donning the robe of a "hanging judge," be as merciful with your mistakes and missteps as you would want others to be with you.

Will it cost you to forgive? Yes, but the cost of unforgiveness is greater.

Will it take courage to forgive? Yes, but the giant leap of courage precedes freedom.

Will it change things? Yes; forgiveness unleashes a healing process and lessens the sting of suffering.

Will it be worthwhile? Yes because unforgiveness is an exhausting beast to manage.

Forgiveness is the most Christ-like action you will ever take, so:

...let go of the need for an apology.

...let go of the need for an explanation.

...let go of the need to hear someone admit his/her wrong.

...let forgiveness flow without expectations.

I promise, there is an unexplainable sense of peace and joy that will fill your soul...as you let go.

Love,

Your Seasoned Self

Read and Reflect

Read Proverbs 19:11, Luke 6:36–37, Luke 7:44–47, Ephesians 4:32, and Colossians 3:13.

What do these Scriptures tell us about God's desire for us to forgive?

_____

_____

_____

_____

Is there anyone you need to forgive? Write a note of forgiveness to them right here right now.

_____

_____

_____

_____

_____

_____

What do you want to tell your younger self about forgiveness?

Dear Younger Me,

_____

_____

_____

_____

_____

_____

_____

_____

_____

_____

_____

_____

_____

_____

_____

_____

Note to Self

Religion

Religious exercise satisfies for a while, but when you encounter and embrace life with Christ and are filled with His Spirit, you will never go back to religion. The day you cross over from a religious life of dos and don'ts to a life yielded to the power of Christ and the guidance of the Holy Spirit is the day when things get real.

Grace becomes real.

Mercy becomes real.

Worship becomes real.

Hope becomes real.

Inner joy becomes real.

Fellowship becomes real.

Expectation becomes real.

God's love becomes real.

Your purpose in life becomes real.

HELP IS HERE

Dear One,

You'll often make this declaration: "I've *got* this."

It's a lie. You won't be able to do life on your own.

So much of life will hinge upon decisions:

Take the job or keep interviewing?

Buy or rent?

Partner with a certain person or don't?

Accept or decline the invitation?

Invest or divest?

Wait or move forward?

Trust or do more research?

Sue in court or let it be?

Since your sight and knowledge are limited, you will need help. You won't find it through a website or an online app or by hiring someone.

Instead, you will need the Helper, the Holy Spirit.

In John 14 and 16, Jesus describes the Holy Spirit as One helping, guiding, comforting, directing, teaching, showing…and so much more.

The Bible refers to the Helper as the Spirit of Wisdom and Revelation. You will need Him, because this world is too complex to navigate in your own strength.

You will find that many people discount a vibrant, ongoing relationship with the Holy Spirit. Because He is the "third person" of the Trinity, they may think that He is ranked third. He's not. The Holy Spirit is co-equal to the Father and the Son, and He knows *you*.

While on Earth, Jesus was limited to the location of His earthly body. That's why He told His disciples: "It is for your good that I am going away. Unless I go away, the Advocate will not come to you; but if I go, I will send him to you" (John 16:7).

Jesus didn't leave people as orphans after His ascension. Instead, He sent the Holy Spirit to live within His followers. If you will invite Him, the Holy Spirit will empower you to live the life to which God has called you.

The Advocate. The Helper. The Holy Spirit.

Jesus *within* you.

If you want to engage the Helper, you must develop a relationship with Him. Talk with Him. Listen for His promptings. Be sensitive and obey what He shows you because it's easy to miss His voice in the busyness of life.

For example, while living in Washington, DC, you will see the same man regularly at a subway exit. Each morning, you will find that it's easy to smile and keep walking.

Then one morning you will encounter a prompting, a gentle inward nudge. It's a holy whisper that "you ought to invite him to coffee."

You certainly wouldn't have thought of that on your own. Excusing yourself, the first thought will be that *the Holy Spirit would* never *ask me to do that*. Again, you will smile and say, "Good morning," but that's as far as it goes.

The whisper will return the next morning.

In the pit of your stomach, you know that if you pass by again, you are willingly disobedient. That's not a good feeling, so you will implore the Helper to give you a boost of bravery while walking over. Extending a hand, you meet Charlie and invite him to breakfast. You're quite a pair, you in your double breasted navy coat and Charlie in his layers of tattered flannel shirts.

It will be the first of several coffees over the next month, special conversations about faith, family, and the consequences of life choices. You will wish him well as he moves south by train to reunite with family.

Each of those meaningful conversations are launched by the Holy Spirit, prompting you to live beyond yourself while giving you courage to act and grace to engage the gentle nudge.

Someone once opined that the Helper speaks in shoulder taps not shouts. It's true. He gently taps us to move in a direction.

The Helper will:

...prompt you to act.

...magnetize you toward a direction.

...prod you from within to respond a certain way, reach out, make a call, write a note, and more.

...impassion you to be more generous, compassionate, and loving than your natural inclinations.

...nudge you to move beyond your comfort zone.

...disquiet you when you're headed toward danger and deception.

...draw you toward God's wisdom and His best.

Being a Christian is not just about learning what's written in the Bible and agreeing with it; it's about living out the Scriptures with the help of the Holy Spirit. Some people wonder what it means to live a "supernatural" Christian life. You will learn that when you partner in relationship with the Helper, His "super" is added to your "natural" limitations. You will also discover that He desires to supply it more often than you realize.

No matter what you're facing, you will never be alone. The Helper will always be there, ready to guide, strengthen, direct, counsel, and comfort. Ask Him to help you. Invite His influence, wisdom, and discernment into each of your days, decisions, and dreams.

Together, you've got this.

Love,

Your Seasoned Self

Read and Reflect

Read John 14–17.

What do these Scriptures tell you about the Holy Spirit?

_____

_____

_____

_____

_____

If you want more of the Holy Spirit's influence and empowerment in your life, take a moment right now and tell Him you would like more of Him.

_____

_____

_____

_____

_____

What do you want to tell your younger self about the importance of relying on the Holy Spirit?

Dear Younger Me,

_____

_____

_____

_____

_____

_____

_____

_____

_____

_____

_____

_____

_____

_____

_____

_____

_____

Note to Self

Your Home, Your Oasis

Create a home environment you look forward to returning
to every day and that provides an oasis for others.
Make your home a welcome place for the Holy Spirit
to dwell. Be careful what you allow into your home.
Protect it with an eye toward anything coming in that
would diminish the sacred presence of the Holy Spirit.

Your bedroom should always be your special place
of peace, a respite from the turmoil of the world.
Words linger in the air, so watch what you are
emitting into the environment with your words.

On the practical side, remember that vacuuming creates
an instant house face-lift, and editing the countertops,
coffee table, and closets of clutter will always be worth
the effort. Keep what you love and let the other stuff
go. Learn to use color—no beige life. You can never
have enough décor pillows. Oh, and plant daffodils and
tulips every fall (in the ground or a container). Every
home needs cut daffodils and tulips in early spring.

WHERE'S THE LOVE?

Dear One,

God's heart is full of affection for you.

In fact, God loves you with the same measure of love He has for Jesus. His love is real, powerful, limitless, and amazing. It's higher, wider, broader, and deeper than you will ever imagine.

You are immensely important to Him.

In His love, He watches over you, sings over you, and rescues you from your enemies.

You'll find that you don't have to perform or earn this love. His love will never be based upon your career or ministry accomplishments. His love won't increase because you check items off your spiritual to-do list. It won't grow with your successes or be diminished by your failures.

God's love does not play favorites. You won't work your way into His heart. His love can't be bought but is simply received and accepted.

He loved you before you received it. Through Jesus Christ, God's love walked the dusty streets of Jerusalem and ultimately paid the penalty for your self-indulgent, sinful rejection of His ways. Yet no one must cleanse him/herself to come into His loving arms. The moment that trust and faith is placed in Jesus, the Savior's merciful and forgiving love washes away the record of the past, beginning a real, life-giving relationship.

At times, you will feel that you've let God down and have lost His love. You haven't. His love is unceasing and steadfast. You will learn to rely on it and rest in it.

At other times, you may hear a lie that He loves others more than you. He doesn't. God's love never rejects. People will say and think wrong things about you. You will say and think wrong things about you. But it's what God says and thinks about you that matters most.

When you are acutely aware of the darkness in your heart, you may think, *How can a holy God love me when I think and act like this?* Dear one, His love is merciful and forgiving.

When your heart is downcast from self-condemnation and bruised from self-loathing, His love heals. It calls you to lift your face to His loving smile.

When you've drifted from fellowship, you may wonder, *Does He still long to know me?* With love, He will always bid you to come to Him.

God will not see you as you see yourself. Instead, He will look at you through His love. While He won't condone wrong actions and motives, He will not withhold his love because of them.

He knows the wounds that will be caused in this world. Yet His love will patiently lead you through seasons of healing, recalibration, and transformation. He is in no rush to fix you. Gently, patiently, and tenderly, as a loving Father, He invites you to align to His thoughts and desires. His love will beckon growth so you will become your best self according to His purposes.

You will see the power of His love. It will move mountains, multiply provisions, stop roaring storms, shepherd you in the wilderness, affirm you at times of self-doubt, and touch you in the deep places unreachable by others.

His love will be far more than a patronizing concern for your welfare. Because of the depth of His love, He will sometimes withhold what you want, giving you more than what was asked or handing you something different. That's because His love is perfect, focused on what's best.

You may run out of food, time, space, patience, ideas, etc., but His love for you will never run dry. It is everlasting and always available. Just come into His presence.

Through meditation on Scriptures, replace any temptation to question God's love. Sing about it and continually reopen your heart for the fresh wind of His love.

Learn about His love, since you will only reflect it to others through your own awareness. Get more and more acquainted with it. Eliminate the lies of doubt that would steer you away from living in its fullness.

If the written word of the Bible could be changed into a single word and become one single voice—this voice more powerful than the roaring of the sea would cry out, "The Father loves you!"

—Saint Augustine

Love,

Your Seasoned Self

Read and Reflect

Read Isaiah 49:16, Romans 8:37–39, 1 John 3:1, 1 John 4:9–10, 1 John 4:16, Hebrews 4:16, and Titus 3:4–5.

What is God speaking to you about His love for you in these Scriptures?

_____

_____

_____

_____

If it is challenging for you to sincerely believe God loves you, just as you are, what are the lies you are believing? Ask Him to break those lies and make His Truth real to you.

_____

_____

_____

_____

_____

What do you want to tell your younger self about why God loves you so very much?

Dear Younger Me,

_____

_____

_____

_____

_____

_____

_____

_____

_____

_____

_____

_____

_____

_____

_____

_____

In My Own Words—A Guide to Mentoring Your Younger Self

It is my hope that reading my letters to my younger self has stirred some thoughts within you about how you want to live your life. One of the things I discovered writing these letters is how faithful God has been to me. It became an exercise of thanksgiving as I reflected on my earlier years of life.

Now that you've had some practice writing to your younger self in response to the themes of this book, I invite you to widen the practice. Space is provided here for you to write your own letters on whatever topics you choose. You may want to write one right away or come back at a later time and write several.

Here are some questions to ponder to help you put pen to paper.

- What lessons might you want to share with your children, grandchildren, or nieces and nephews through a letter to your younger self?
- How could you give God thanks for the things He has shown you or brought you through by writing a letter to your younger self?
- If you met with your younger self for thirty minutes over coffee, what would you say? How would you

encourage him/her? What cautions would you express?

- Is there a particular season of your life you would counsel your younger self through?

Grab a cup of coffee and a nice pen and start writing. Don't try to write perfectly. Just be honest, be genuine, and let your thoughts and words flow.

If you would like to share a letter, I would be honored to read it and celebrate with you what you have learned.

Growing with you,

— *Michelle*

michelle@michellehoverson.com

Dear _____,

_____

_____

_____

_____

_____

_____

_____

_____

_____

_____

_____

_____

_____

_____

_____

_____

Dear _____,

_____

_____

_____

_____

_____

_____

_____

_____

_____

_____

_____

_____

_____

_____

_____

_____

_____

_____

_____

Dear _____,

Dear _____,

_____

_____

_____

_____

_____

_____

_____

_____

_____

_____

_____

_____

_____

_____

_____

_____

_____

Dear _____,

Dear _____,

_____

_____

_____

_____

_____

_____

_____

_____

_____

_____

_____

_____

_____

_____

_____

_____

A Word about Above & Beyond

Who we are

Above & Beyond is a faith-based missions foundation dedicated to ending spiritual poverty by helping people earn funds for short-term missions assignments. Through an innovative *Serve Local Go Global* program, short-term missionaries are financially rewarded for serving their neighbors so they may go serve people in other nations. Above & Beyond global messengers begin their missionary journey at home.

Why we exist

When Jesus gave us the Great Commission, He invited us to live above and beyond just believing in Him. He called us to go and tell. Despite the church's efforts, half the people on earth have never heard the gospel message. Through Above & Beyond's unique funding model, short-term missionaries called to go can say yes when facing financial obstacles.

Who we impact

As of 2019, Above & Beyond has assisted over 1,200 short-term missionaries who have invested over 18,000 volunteer hours in their local communities before sharing the gospel with people in eighty-seven nations.

When an Above & Beyond applicant receives an award, nonprofits gain a volunteer, a global ministry is strengthened, a missionary receives valuable funding, and Christ is made known.

What you can do

Send: Some are called to go, and others are able to send. Your monthly sponsorship or legacy gift will help an Above & Beyond applicant be a global messenger through mission teams providing medical clinics, orphanage support, youth outreaches, leadership training, church construction, and other forms of spiritual nurture. Supporting the *Serve Local Go Global* program also increases volunteerism in local communities. Visit www.AboveandBeyondMissions.org for more information and to read testimonies from Above & Beyond recipients.

Pray: Above & Beyond continually needs prayer for perseverance, favor, and creativity.

Invite: Given that a portion of the proceeds from this book will be given to Above & Beyond, Michelle would welcome the opportunity to speak at a book club, women's ministry, missions conference, or other event.

Thank You!

I hope you have been blessed by this book. If you would like to be notified of future podcasts or updated content, please sign up at http://www.michellehoverson.com/book-bonus.

Please do not hesitate to connect with me if you have any questions about this book or if you would like to share one of your letters to your younger self with me. I'd love to see what you wrote and connect with you.

If you enjoyed this book, may I ask you for a quick favor? Please leave the book a review on Amazon. Reviews are very important for authors. I promise it doesn't take very long and it will help this book reach more readers like you.

Thank you so much for reading my letters and for allowing me to spend a mentoring moment with you.

—Michelle

About the Author

Michelle Hoverson is currently the executive director of Above & Beyond, a missions foundation dedicated to seeing the end of spiritual poverty. Above & Beyond's *Serve Local Go Global* program has assisted thousands of short-term missionaries to earn mission trip funding. Because of Michelle's commitment to mobilizing people to local and global outreach, a portion of the proceeds of this book will go to Above & Beyond.

Prior to serving at Above & Beyond in her current role, Michelle had a pastoral career that spanned twenty-three years at two different churches. At Grace Covenant in Cornelius, North Carolina, she served as the associate pastor for global and local compassion ministries for sixteen years. Her other pastoral position was at Capital

Church in McLean, Virginia. Ordained by the International Foursquare Church, her season in pastoral positions was preceded by many years in various corporate communication positions, including roles with an international law firm, an advertising agency, and a commercial real estate developer. Shortly after graduating from Washington College, Michelle had the honor of serving our nation in a White House position.

Michelle is driven by a passion to see every person who is created in the image of God have a vibrant relationship with the One who created them. As she has led over fifty mission teams to multiple nations, taught hundreds of classes, and spoken at conferences, her motivating hope has been to help people believe, at a deep heart level, that God loves them and encourage them to have an authentic relationship with Jesus Christ.

Michelle and her husband, Walt, live outside Charlotte, North Carolina. They have three adult children. In addition to their natural siblings, Walt and Michelle have hundreds of cherished brothers and sisters around the world. You can connect with Michelle at mhoverson@ AboveandMissions.org or through Linkedin.com/in/ michellehoverson.